In the Crocodile Gardens
poems

More works by Saba Syed Razvi:

Of the Divining and the Dead (Finishing Line Press)

Limerence (Chax Press)

In the Crocodile Gardens
poems

Saba Syed Razvi

Agape Editions
Los Angeles, CA

Published by Agape Editions
http://agapeditions.com
Los Angeles, CA

Agape Editions is an imprint of Sundress Publications.

Copyright © 2016 by Saba Syed Razvi
All rights reserved

Cover image: *Eater of Hearts*, by Carrie Ann Baade
Egg tempera and oil on canvas, 2007
Used by kind permission of the artist

Cover design: Lauren A. Pirosko
Book design: Lauren A. Pirosko

Editor: Fox Frazier-Foley

Editorial Intern: Jasmine An

Library of Congress
Cataloguing-in-Publication Data
In the Crocodile Gardens // Saba Syed Razvi
Library of Congress Control Number 2015959455
Razvi, Saba Syed
ISBN 978-1-939675-30-9

9 8 7 6 5 4 3 2 1

FIRST EDITION

Table of Contents

Chalked Circles and Circumferences of Breath	1
Amphibious Catalogue with Invisible Stair, Or The Malady of Melusine	2
In the crocodile gardens,	3
Demon: Lover	4
A Lover's Quarrel	5
Gilded	6
Snow Song	7
Promise	8
Poisonfruit	9
Once	10
Michelangelo's Ex	11
In Looking Back	12
Predatory	13
Meditation After a Lost Battle: Curatorial Statements for a Museum Exhibit	15
For the Benefit of the Cartographer's Fire	16
American Dream with Horizon and Pomegranate, O Dervish of the Restless Heart	17
Fossil Before the Making	18
Ever Aftering	19
Curse of the Elders: A Caution Against Mystery	20
Like Red, Dancing for the Wolf	21
Oil Field. Mine, field. Afghanistan.	22
Beware: Crocodiles, Do Not Feed the Ducks	23
Aggregate	24
Through Albatross Eyes	25
The Hour of Waiting Windows	26
Shock & Awe	27
Blue Heron,	28
Thisbe, Upon Seeing the Lion	29
Hyenas	30
The Key Club	31
Psyche in Love	32
Prophetstown, IL	33
Siren Song	34
Persephone to Orpheus	35
A Poultice for the Reckoner of Time and Seasons	36
Apology from a Split Morrow	37
A Measure of Thirst and Topiary	38

Out of Clay and Back Again	39
Mercy from the Red Queen	40
Morning Unexpectedly Sapphic	41
Evening, Fireside	42
Morning After	43
The Marquis Slips into an Understanding	44
Aubade for an Absent Lover, or From the Asphodel Fields	45
Ligeia's Despair	46
Bachelorettes	47
Her Door Slamming in the Middle of the Longest Night	48
From Inside the Painted Window Frame	49
Before Solomon's Court	51
Lovesick Wanderer, O Dervish of the Restless Heart	52
Exile	53
A Swallow of Gravity	54
Talisman	55
The Reptile's Wife	56
Animus: the Hierophant and the Hetaira	57
Swampfed Lullaby	58
Fury	59
Found Song	60
Longing Along the Long Winter's Eve	61
Persephone in the Nights of Spring	62
Scrying for the Unworthy with Feather and Bone and Sanctuary	63
Shade in the Telesterion, from Beyond the Mystery Rites of Eleusis in Spring	64
Aubade for a Seraph (or a Demon)	68
Dream with Astrolabe and Compass	69
The Wanderer's Compass is a Quest to Find the House of God	70
Mirror Lake in Carlsbad Cavern Quivers Like a Scrying Glass Speaking	71
Self-Portrait as Wick-Tender and Candle Flame	72
Anthem for the Ancestors, O Dervish of the Restless Heart	73
But for the Garden is the Guardian Ravenous	75
Nor Equinox Nor Promise	76
References and Notes	79
Acknowledgements	85
About the Author	89
A Note on the Type	91
A Note on the Setting of the Type	92

This book is for my father,
who taught me how to love the world and all of its mysteries,
and who left this world loved by all who knew him.

"Beneath English trees I meditated on that lost maze: I imagined it inviolate and perfect at the secret crest of a mountain…I thought of a labyrinth of labyrinths, of one sinuous spreading labyrinth that would encompass the past and the future and in some way involve the stars. Absorbed in these illusory images, I forgot my destiny of one pursued. I felt myself to be, for an unknown period of time, an abstract perceiver of the world…The afternoon was intimate, infinite. The road descended and forked among the now confused meadows. A high-pitched, almost syllabic music approached and receded in the shifting of the wind, dimmed by leaves and distance. I thought that a man can be an enemy of other men, of the moments of other men, but not of a country: not of fireflies, words, gardens…"
—Jorge Luis Borges, "The Garden of Forking Paths."

"This island is governed by kings. These princes profess to be sons of crocodiles, that is issued from the highest origin to which human beings can claim. Accordingly, these scaly ancestors abound in the island's rivers, and are the subject of a particular veneration. They are protected, they are spoilt, they are adulated, they are fed, they are offered young maidens as fodder—and ill-fortune to the foreigner who lays a hand on the sacred lizards."
—Jules Verne, *Twenty Thousand Leagues Under the Sea.*

"That mine of sweetness is what I desire. To settle for fate is to trifle with bread and water. I am a fish. To battle a crocodile is what I desire."
—Rumi.

"The one who sleeps in the midst of a garden longs to be awakened. But, for the one who sleeps in a prison, to be awakened is a nuisance."
—Rumi.

Chalked Circles and Circumferences of Breath

Go as far north as you can and find snow

Go as far south as you can and find snow

Go as far east as you can Go and it becomes west again, far back as where you began.

Find me a shelf of colored bottles, a votive for a lovèd's grave, a silent room with tables for a hot cup or a clean glass.

Find me a colorless flag full of flagpoles mined from every step between, threaded, knotted as many times as steps.

I would not walk 10,000 miles, coming back to another start of ten thousand miles, miles around the world until home is home again.

Along this way, onward this way, the air reddens, purples, blues into darkness curving all-around, a tunnel leaving only the path as far as I can expel a light, spotlight, pocket, long wail of longing for sleep.

Find me a sheaf of colored pages, a bloom for the baby's crib, a silent room with a warm cup, with tables.

Go as far east as you can Go and it becomes a star, becomes west again, far back as where it began.

Go as far south as you can Go and find snow

Go as far north as you can Go and find snow

At a curve of miles onto miles, find me.

Amphibious Catalogue with Invisible Stair, Or The Malady of Melusine

I have been standing here a long time at this shoreline in the valley of the singing fishes. The paint of my toenails has chipped. They surface, from time to time, sucking at my toes when teething and the polish breaks away in flakes on their newling teeth. They are green as vetiver or a new moon and sometimes, yellow, sick with desire or a premonition of death. I will stand here until my toes are gone, nibbled away by the iridescent-eyed, scaled bodies because there is littlewhere left to go. Whither do I wander, wondering, whether anything is lost. When they are hungry, the waves purple, dusking into a deeper calm. The river is violet often, never violent enough to blacken or crest and it can be unnerving standing at the edge of something sometimes stream and sometimes sea. I like to name them, but they rebel and even my most faithful visitors will vanish once I call them by a Samuel, Solomon, or Barnaby. It is as if to say: what is hidden is always beautiful, the found never. I was looking for a death orchard in a flat blank plain and found instead a fountain of shadow, and it led me here beneath the crescent night. If I grow a tail, may I be a mermaid, then?

In the crocodile gardens,

my teeth line the killing field—
glowing orbs hover, each of
a molten light wound like wet string—
where I planted sun seeds on a morning,
on my tongue.

I prefer my moments to be outside of time.

A wormhole is a hole
inside the soil where
light or lightless lack
matters not
to a field of nascent suns.

Demon : Lover

Ever it begins

by the blue water and the convulsing
of your bones
breaking
to be free of your flesh, freer than—

take it in—

greener, sweeter than
these vines,
the shadow of the Spanish Moss
and its tender-rills sun-spilt
over your mouth—

take it in—

this kiss,
water-wet and ether.

Ever. And never. It begun

by locks of long black,
like beckoning fingers in this breeze,
the shadow of the swimming eel
in the stream.

A Lover's Quarrel

I'll be Pierrot and you—Columbine in a red sash,
in a velvet suit, in a lamplit halo of a hat—

> *Tell me something True?*

I was looking for my love in a pixel gallery when the red of 113
days and one year blushed bold across my keystroke thumb—

> *Was it magic? Was it mood?*

And we can find a Mardis Gras on a beaded walk of pebbles,
on a garden filled with only imperfect blooms—for the sin
eater's table spread!—

> *If you wish?*

We found a screech of such a convoluted construction, through
a pointer and a wave, that it snapped—your mouth wide, your throat
closed, a moment like a stone found in your cream—

> *Would you take Toast & Tea?*

My lips were ivory, clenched to keep my teeth from snapping
through each and another—

> *If I don't move, will I always look
> to you the same?*

Or—you can be Pierrot and I'll pose as a columbine, androgyne
or gamine, with a sometimes-severed tongue and fingers illumined
in a glittered clench or ringed in streaks of remaindered paint

Gilded

My lover's thumb fits exactly
along the contour of my cheekbone—
we are one
species, the same, and I am
sick of long-stemmed, orange blossoms
beside the bedside table—uniform
of offering, still. I am sick
of days unraveling into undone tapestries.

Turn me orange as gold, turn me
scaled and sequined, shimmering
like a dying fish
because to gasp is a way of stealing
a slipping life, a way of wanting
to hold on to what is not, still.

Turn me winged as a golden oriole,
song-bellied, song-belied, and rising
from still slumber into the dark—arms
wide as wind.

Snow Song

A wolf's eyes know the jagged terrain of winter,
Like an uncut path

They can discern a snowfall from the tallest peaks,
The slightest shift of white

You are anything but a wolf
Howl, in the Siberian sky, anything
But the anguish of an unspoken wish

A wolf's eyes are not hungry, but eager,
Mistaken often by men who know
Less of paws than of songs of paws

I know your name by the fir
And pine,
The acorn-smelling air at dusk

And your eyes are yellow,
Tuneless as a black dream unsung in the soil.

Promise

Loveless Thisbe, do not mistake the sound
of a voice through the wall for a voice that seeks
a home inside the walls
of *your* heart.
Every voice echoes.
And there are other chambers less like stone
or crumbling gate, with open doors into their rooms,
with unbarred windows.
What you touch is no more
than the shadow of your hand against your palm.
A hand on the other side of the wall is free
to hold or not hold itself against the farther side,
to say it touches back, whether unfelt or untrue.

Poisonfruit

Seduce me with an apple or a pome,
I will laugh for you—
archetype and nothing more; do you
think that it is sweet,
what I crave?
Wrong-fleshed choice.
Desire, too, has a shadow,
and it hungers.

I am no goddess—no kindness in me—
to be won.

Once

A night in paper
shapes of light, when full
of too much
honeyed color, I
reached up and you, holding
my waist with one hand, stretched
and plucked for me the yellowest
lemons, dropping them unseen
into my upturned hand.
The leaves,
higher than my halo of breath, still
inside yours.

Now, the trees are cut
to rooted stumps.
I reach up
To amputated branches, just
as blank
as if you'd never felt green
for me, before.

Michelangelo's Ex

Nights beside the water,
she watches
statues.

Pale unmoving
forms, liquid under shadows—
here was a slight smile, there
a colored iris, a question inside
that frown.
He is marble.
His stone features can break.

She makes hollow men
to love; one, another, an army,
who will always
remain.

In Looking Back

Hero, you have left me
to rescue myself
from the simple cave
I entered, falling behind
your shadow.

The spider weaves her sticky strands
at the mouth—
to catch around my ankles, bound—
my hands, my feet to your certain words.

My bones could break
through the soil,
into the threshold of the sun,
my toe past a perimeter of heavy dust.

Still, you will not remember,
to believe more than your shadow
moves behind you.

Predatory

A velveteen sheaf in Tyrian blue on the table and
on it, an assortment of holes and feathers, and
on it an assemblage of glittering shells,
not to steal the moment of death but still its onset for a brief few hours, and
on it the price of risk.
He worries.
Each mask has lived a lifetime
in the shopkeeper's hands, waits now to try its charm.
What if…[*Everything will fall again*]

onto the stiff cobblestone walk, if I don't do this again,
adjust, again, adjust, again like this, and
[*leave me alone,*]
to keep this safe on our display.
He tells her, *go now to the side there*
where the wind might drop off,
a piece or two of pretty prices in an instant.
He hurries. Shifting, between tables at his booth,
he turns to her, question for a question, [*Annie, would I lie to you?*]

and lying beneath the table at the front corner is an empty space,
a blue like a curtain for me to slip under
to see from under,
to watch the walking feet from under
and the hands with small things swinging in transit and in talk.
I take it.
What a perfect cover for a thief, for me,
for a man in brown fading into the shade of ground.
Quick as a brown fox.
Waiting for someone to ask [*How long have you been lost down here?*]

to caterwaul from color
into my desire to take,
for any thing unlike a thing that announces itself as nothing but itself.
And here a hookah made of ivory and glinting glass, not inlay but a paint.
A desire to break it. Nothing more.
And here a skirt so tight she cannot walk, even
on her legs like stalks of egret limb.
Her fully pantalooned friend says [*Gimme the scissor, hammer, flame*]

and I can make you a better bit of glass than that
marbling box on the box-shaped table.
Beside the girl, he is clumsy in his stride.
A desire to break her. Legs, nothing more.
A chair of fading wood, faded yellow brocade tapestried to the top.
Plastic bags. Of marbles. Yes, colored marbles. Tied
to the rungs between the legs. Small feet walking to *Now?* [*How soon is now?*]

And can we open them now? Or now? Then,
fast feet in heavy heels before the stiletto heels wobbling between the stones,
a pair, two pairs of feet. Wobbling beneath warbling high voices.
Orange fingernails holding in one hand a hat made of green Chinese silk
in the shape of a cylinder,
stopping at the table under which I am. Her friend. In red velvet Mary Janes
complains, [*How could I be so immature to think*
that he could replace the missing element in me? How extremely lazy of me!]

Slippers!
And she angles one foot against the other, lays one over the other.
A dancer.
Ballet shoes in blood red bold, nothing like the blush of modest pink
and pale abalone.
How about this mask?, her friend orangely asks.
No, but this one has perfect blue feathers. Like sky.
The shopkeeper's voice after she leaves, high like shivering branches and I
slip out behind their talk of [*what if*
all these fantasies come flailing down? Oh no. I've said too much.]

stealthing behind their stillettoed feet.
Now she holds the mask to her face, hidden behind bright plumage.
A feather! When she drops her hand, I will pluck just one streak of sleeping
turquoise.

Meditation After a Lost Battle: Curatorial Statements for A Museum Exhibit

1.
The warrior in the drum
folds and stretches iron
in longing.
He wears
a necklace of human bone.
He wears
a swordsman's calm
in his still, set mouth.
He is armored.

2.
The warrior drums in
the stretching sword,
folding and unfolding,
unhandled and molten.
He is a mandala.
He wears a necklace
from a ritual apron of bone.
He is human in a beating hand,
heart like an open drum

0.
mandala

3.
The mandala in the warrior
throbs like a drum.
His heart bears
a sword.
His sword bears
her name.
He wears around his neck
her
Beaded bones, unfolding down
along his waist, still.

4.
The mouth of the drum in the
mandala throbs,
folding and yielding open
into a handle of human
bone.
Between the hand and the heart
is a blade,
sheeted still from mandarin-hot iron.
Her heart is bone.
The warrior's neck, unarmored

For the Benefit of the Cartographer's Fire

"For the true American appears to be ashamed to say anything in the way it has been said before." – Mina Loy.

1. State of the Word

You might be pleased to hear that we don't talk of tea much, but like to have a Latte or a Caffeine Fix or a Cup of Joe. You might not mind that the Trinidadian "dropping words" is brighter than the way Americans "talk trash," but would you mind that all the gossip is gossiped in the same world's words? Nothing novel or new, and normally in the same café that greets you at every corner in the same words. When did Americans delight in using words with wit and discretion for a new world? When did the words of the speaker's creation begin to emerge from a lack and not a love of what has not been said before? He drops his words, not deliberately, but clumsily, like his mouth is full of too much pretzel. Would this innovation be called American, too?

2. State of Novelty

Once, to be American was visionary. To be open, to imagine, to explore. Is it still? I follow your hand's length this far and not that, this way and stopping now, but my reach does not change your grasp. Your bright lines and angles stretched skyward, filled the blank with shape, and you loved them. You lent your own body's surfaces to such a building. Upwards moves now, too, progressing wider, but samely. Is it the same to move as to move anew?

3. State of My Self

Thinking myself uncorseted, I spoke a word I had not known until then. In a picture of a woman hiding in a corner, you saw not her eyes, but a chance to make another picture. A woman in her eyeliner, in a flag as a veil. Was it a breaking open of a freer word, or a hemming in, thereof.

4. State of Action

For the true American is ashamed when he says nothing that was not said before. Anymore. A step can say as much, a boot, a marching band of boots as loud as bodied voices speaking disembodied words, said before. A shot can say as much as a scream, a siren or a single burst overhead and then a refrain of the same, echoing. The voice that speaks apart is not a voice, is not speaking in a language that is of here. A difference in language can be incorporated, but in truth, it is ignored.

American Dream with Pomegranate and Horizon, O Dervish of the Restless Heart

(On the occasion of the departure of forces, US and NATO, after twelve years of war in Afghanistan)

In the water of the scrying bowl, strings of silver curl into the letters of some foreign alphabet, letters formed of smoke and fog, of sand and kohl, palimpsests, of fire, fireless flame, firefly shame, starlight and otherworldly breath, pluming in the cold of desertscapes. // I dream you, fatigued, in fatigues, flesh charred, but in tact, singed and covered in soot, but alert and alive, more stunned than bled, your eyes, smiling—luminous, bright and blue as a drone-ready sky. // I dream you gathering seeds in the land of pomegranates, scattering them along the mountainsides, the sandy dunes, the horizon like a lion's mane curling as the beast startles into some readied stance. // And, as I miss your fingers tracing the language of my lost tongue along my skin, the words I do not know, bursting into lush green life inside me, fire and flame and flower petals the color of spring. // I dream you safe and crossing currents of air and smoke toward an unsettled home, a waiting home, your hand scattering those gathered seeds with an open hand. And, when is April like a bride in Spring, the cypresses scenting the breeze? // I dream that they sprout flesh along barren terrain left behind, hearts, beating fruit, budding with fear and with frustration, with the anticipation of a coming storm.

Fossil Before the Making

Dearest Monster—last night I slept
in the ozone-scented stratosphere,
waking to the lurch and hum of a great
mechanical wing, over sea. Unfurling
and retreating the way a pterodactyl's
crinolined appendage once hushed
the Vulcan burst of earth, it silenced my
protest against a morning
inside the belly of an aluminum bird.
Around me, rows of dim, upright teeth
and, in place of one, I. Had I woken
from within enamel shell, cracking
against my sinew, tautening tense?
This light grows brighter, but it does not
call me home—it fixes me, still—Yours.

Ever Aftering

Dearest Madness,
You are not what I choose, but what I cannot
turn away. The sheer wings of Bluest Morpho,
morphose into peacock feather pattern, into a
single flap of skin left hanging on my skeleton.
Will you not come to me across the miles?
Your—

                        Are you mine, Muse?
That shielding my windows mightn't keep you
away? I dreamt of you again, and woke with
the lull of bagpipes in my hair, my skin sore, as
if it had been peeled and pulled back into place.
Tell me, then, what you demand.
                                 Waiting Here.

Dear Mitochondria,
I will call you something that I crave until I find
a something else to live by. Writing to you on an
antique fainting couch in velvet, everything sinks.
This morning howled open, as from nightmare and
Jasmine bloom. Aren't the evenings purple anymore?
Yours.

          And what you crave is a child, then, rumpled
Rumplestiltzkin?
This is a tricky game. Perhaps you know something
that I have not touched yet? Tell me what it is. I am,
                              dying to know.

Curse of the Elders: A Caution Against Mystery

do not dig here, where the quartz protrudes,
long fingers like old fingers, unclutched.
do not dig here where the cracks of earth are
filled, with once-red blood. clay, in the stone,
and in the soil, and in the sun, baking
like earthen bread, they stood once, fallen now
into lines. there is danger in the wood, in this
brooding earth. only wires carrying fire can
still traverse the submerged bones. do not dig
here where the wires like snakes will sting,
will poison with sparked tongues unattached
to coiled vine body. no story lies here waiting
to be told. only, do not dig here, but elsewhere
in the burying earth.

Like Red, Dancing for the Wolf

a thousand peacocks' eyes couldn't watch me sane
couldn't wash the reflection of you from my lidless dreams

in a bed, in a box, is waiting
in birdsong, in bricks, is building

a thousand mornings couldn't breathe me safe
couldn't kill the guillotine glint in your incisors or your anger

in a corset, in a quiet room, is velocity
in a skin-cut, in a whip-sting, is violane

a thousand legs to carry me home
       and a millipede's petal-quenched wish
would carry me dancing boot-heeled back—
       your jaws, pink-tongued

Oil field. Mine, field. Afghanistan.

Workers below do not work to throw rocks or other missiles.
Workers below are pelted with rocks and other missiles.
Workers before sometimes bulldozed, preventing future missiles,
and un-misled voices, standing guard against the door to home,
scraped away the bones of the unloving and unloved.

No man that is not man needs a guard, no-man
is man that is bluffed by missile. Noman is man that has
become nomad, in tents and graveyards, where a plastered poster's
picture depicts how to tie a tourniquet when no-man nomad
has stepped through not a missile's arc but a mine-field.

Once, here, were pomegranate trees, once whooping birds and
Jasmines big as a fist, until a fist took,
shook fistfuls into sand and caves and sand replaced the places
where missiles later sought and demanded misled bones,
bones like those fleshed bones standing in front of bulldozers.

Beware: Crocodiles, Do Not Feed The Ducks.

The crocodiles move faster than you
think: waddling sluggish as heat-waves
they could not catch the body among waves
turbulent and thick.
                      They bask, waiting, like
thieves in ambush, seeking the right flailing
hand to snatch from under the shadow of sun.
Raise up your hands
                    like that, in repetitive
motion, and scatter breadcrumbs to the stagnant
tide: you will bring forth an armada
                            of ducks
and beneath their hoarse quacks, the stealthy
pad of reptile, out of bayou, river, and swamp,
having arrived at your flagrant wave
of meaty arm, an invitation to lunch.

Aggregate

Hello dear futurebaby, curled up like a lapis lizard, lazuli as blue and flecked with gold in my mind's third eye. I can see your fast, full beating heart inflating and deflating your unformed ribcage right against the left window of my sight. Citing your feat, my dreams know to tell you not to worry, that my long black cat, bonier than Bast, will neither eat you nor carry you on his pink tongue, that his mouth remains closed from you except to make you a new sound. Sound as a bell you are, still in the far belly of a violet light. Light your unshed gills on fire, darling, and spread like quickest silver through my eyelids, through the inside of my irises so that even in seeing beyond you, I might still see you, and know that you are mined.

Through Albatross Eyes

Perhaps there are things in the unforgiving arctic
ice beside the frozen hearts of mammoths,
enormous tusks curving like scythes

left behind by stray wanderers.
In the ice underfoot, a necklace made
of walrus tusk, an anklet of
brittle fishbone.

Only a winter sky could rival
so much blue: slated
balance of water and ice,
stormcloud and wind.

Here the ground will not relent, even
for bootprints and feet,
here is the history of time
in each stilled drop of water.

The Hour of Waiting Windows

Corvid creature, can you not
sing your cawing screech into my long-listening ear?

word the wordless minstrel
so long lost to sight without an echo?

feather me with your winged eves and break them
into storm-split syllables, pressing against the panes?

Shock & Awe

That sound cannot be real—but it is, bursting
over Baghdad. Bombs over Baghdad. Everything
turning inward, to ash,
blood, bodies, bricks—now fumes
spreading the way dye blossoms
in a jar of water, reddening in my hands,
or a burst capillary opens
across the white canvas of cornea. My eyes
cannot be turned, my face
damp with the loss I have
never met.   I do not wear a veil
everyday, but today in defiance.
From my kitchen the small heat
of a gas stove—how could I even remember
to scream, if the flume of blue kept growing?

Blue Heron,

how can you stand so—

poised on one leg, as if to say:

two is cumbersome?

Thisbe, Upon Seeing the Lion

The sphinx is red and like a succubus
desires
to be filled with anxious breath.

The moment of arched back, broken-
waisted defeat
reveals
the torso
of a feline, sinewed and fanged and
claws parting the sheaf of skin
down her rigid spine.

What the riddle answers is stolen, a wish inside
the sphinx's kiss.
What the night sees is a roar, a bloody pair of lips.

Hyenas
(after William Carlos Williams)

laughing to each other in the night
& we

lock the doors,
call our loves in to the lit walled light.

In the morning,
no sound

heralds the hatching sun
but blood—

spilt red against white feathers—
congeals in the raided chicken coop.

The Key Club

Approach the door in my tall, white
dress and glass
slippers. And a man, black in denim,
stands to block my way, silent,
as if to see me,
as if to say, "I know your kind
and this is not your place."
Behind me, a woman shouts through
a megaphone, a man shouts through
a megaphone, and their words are folded
in echo. Then music, riotous, Rage Against
The Machine, without a vocalist. There
is protest in the park. I stand swaying.
On stiletto heels of ice,
I have walked through water. He says,
"You know that story
with the pumpkins; it wasn't true."

Psyche in Love

The stairs of spine lead
not to where you have come
but to where you should have
begun.

A woman with a free heart
& a free soul
is always left
a *hetaira*—
unowned,
unpossessed in waiting.

It is she
who recognizes her cage
of bones for what it is,
her body—
a temple of bones—
who can claim sanctuary
in the sacred—
this, too, unowned.

Prophetstown, IL

It is like the way you feel, driving too fast
on a long highway,
road slipping discretely below the hem
of the upturned sky,

like this road might lead all the way
past Kerouac's wind-faded footprints,
out to where the coast opens before you,
holding salt in its curling water-fingers,

or else into the flatlands where
one sky looks only like another
and there is no exit.

After too many unfamiliar city
limits, you might begin to wish
for your own Penelope—
not desire, not love,
just somewhere to belong;
it is
the journey that steals and replaces you,
leaves knots in place of gut and only words
in the songs surfacing
through peaks of static on the radio.

Siren Song

Why am I so eager to break again
onto you as the surf onto itself,
carried by the weight of its own desire
for an end

that turns again to unbeginning? In
the beginning there was no light and in
the end will be the darkness after light
has splintered

into the colors of birth. To be born
of the sea is to ascend from shark's teeth,
in rows like corn or coral. To be born
of the sea

is to remember a time without sun,
where clay rests on fire. Carry me back
to the ocean when I cannot walk there
anymore,

carry me into the relentless tide,
unwilling
to relinquish its hunger, to let go.

Persephone to Orpheus

The feverish pulp of your heart
is not enough an offering—
it is your voice that I want.

Echoes burst against the stone,
fireworks in my ears
racing swift along the canyon edge
splitting death and life—
when will your throat dry?

Relinquish what is mine.

A Poultice for the Reckoner of Time and Seasons

a pile of pickled bats and porcupine quills and a half-
dead, decaying baby bird in the pine needles I swept
off the balcony—
a marionette who's lost its wings, its strings
and I would make a nest of all the unfinished
letters filling up a sheaf of mine bookshelf entire—
but my circuits are burnt
and dust-curdling—
am I Prada, *prêt a porte,* postmodern sleazy?
Moby maybe of a best-sell breakfasted morning, oh—
who can bear to unburden a secret, love? tell me
a dream, my darkest,
oh, my darkling—
is my lover more than just a word, a just word, world,
from whom I inherit a bedscape of feathers and feather-
less wings?

Apology from a Split Morrow

        blue tattoo flowers / boxes of perfume
clouds of petal and attar and rose, made of sand, of skin /
        the unspun skin / a blooming vessel
        a bowl on the table / full of cream
and a drop / red clot / reddening outward like a birdsong
        the window/ blossoms of foxfire / the breeze
a bird's wing / ink / the shadow and the shade on the table /
    altar and spilt salt, swimming in the curdling cream
        bright stones / begging to adorn the blue
skin-flowers / bright, bezzled gems/ gold-flecked blue.

A Measure of Thirst and Topiary

At the end of a long thread, my throat opens, mouth tilting wide, head tipping back for the single drop that the Queen of Cups is willing to give me from the curve of her fingernail.

In a white room, the walls are made of lights, she is drifting on a cushion on a carpet of opulence, with jet black and eggshell white ostrich feathers crowning her shadowblack hair.

I can see nothing more of her but the pink of her mouth against the plumage.

In acres of organza, she might have once slept with lions—*la belle et la bête*—a carpet of jungle tresses and bursting orchids, a lagoon whispering a Narcissan compliant, complaint of birds.

Here, she cups her elegant fingers from the stalk of a thin wrist above the pool, hands dripping now with a stream, now shimmering with beads, each to lull the beast beside her waist, whose long mane carpets her toes, her thighs, her heavy breasts when she unhinges

her jaws in the silence of a roar, spilling stream-song by globes of fluid prism onto the points of her own sharp teeth and the pointed tip of her greedy tongue.

Out of Clay and Back Again, What am I?

Bottle brittle, bottle bare,
bottle me up with a fair-
haired maiden in the sea
and send me silverly

into the

Green foam, sea foam, undrentide,
promise me that valentine
will hold the stitches in the heart
and break it with the cold stone part

of seashell splinter
by the colored sea.

Cinder, sand, and driftwood,
call the rabbit from the moon to me,
the Aztec courage in the globe,
volcano-driven, fire-grown.

Abalone, pink and green,
shimmer in the shellèd night.
Slivers, fit in skin to find
the scarred rings of jellytree.

Here a jellyfish on the sand,
placental pink and tendril and
a song of stinging,
like the voice of the oldest man

and the wrongest tree.

There a sharp stone in the hand
to burst the fishfruit over land
and spill the sticky residue
of fingerlust, of silent tongue,

of eggy birth from gill to lung,
from the ballast of the vessel into be—

Bottle brittle, bottle bare,
bottle me up with fair-
haired mermen sunning on a jetty
by the slumbering tidalled sea.

Mercy from the Red Queen

Oh, and how could I deny her?
With those eyes like Lorca's women,
in her Alberta Ferretti dress,
I would have killed Venus,
brought back skin for powder.
I would have eaten poinsettias
if my lips weren't red enough
for her design. I watched her
swing beneath the laziest
branch, her toes
dragging shapes along the dust.
Nor did she grace me with one smile,
nor one glance of honest iris.
Those teeth guarded words
not meant to be said.
So, I brought her tongues,
with which to speak to me,
casting aside lips blanched pale with begging,
falling into wordheld casts for reading by, for
in those eyes was wanting.

Morning Unexpectedly Sapphic

Stretched supine on a mat,
watching you, she is
playing the oldest game:
she loves me, she loves me not.
Between the hardened leaf
of painted fingernail—the softest
petals. Your breath is small,
the rise and fall of your breasts
is small. But each exacts
a tug of blossom slipping
away from stem, leaving plain
a core. Oh, Kore, she is not bound,
like you, inhaling
you, to continue with
any other iris; and with no silent
sound can dull the pace of quickening
stroke. She will not let you wake
to her in this room
ripe with the smell of bananas
when all she wants is a peach.

Evening, fireside.

Given the heft of this hand cupped around your full breast, should not, should not your husband know the weight of your, wait of your, desire? Should, shoulder the knot behind your navel unwind, in river in riven in rift of the song? Rougher than your husband, hand calloused, his hand callous his heart, his hard, his whore's mind for the want of the weary of your waiting, weighted sex. Your body coiling, smoke, like smoke among the heart of the hearth. Is the night so long away that the sun lingers in wait? Is your cup in your own soft hands full of the leaves of tea, milkthistle and mead, leaving you the shapes of language, lingering, hatchling green, on your tongue? A tongue to linger along the cup, the lap, the foretold song.

Morning After

Just past the green tines of trees
pointing into gradations
of indigo—a satellite blinking,
or a planet, a plane.
Dare I make a transient's wish?
There is nothing still untethered
that can yield.

The Marquis Slips into an Understanding

He remembered her in the starlight, hands bound behind her.
She sat, on knees, draped only in long hair, hung like whips of willow
dripping over stoic eyes, a chastity belt, a glass key hung around her neck.

And he thought *anhedoniac*
And she thought *redemption*

He remembered her scars like spider-webs clinging to the skin of her back,
slits at her shoulder blades where once might grow wings.

And he thought *her magic gone*
And she thought *this silent warmth growing in my belly*

She hung her head when light sharper than blades, exposed her,
longing for the violet of twilight sky.

And he thought *prayer*
And she thought *retribution*

Aubade for an Absent Lover, or, from the Asphodel Fields

Fever dreams birth the strangest
goblins—metallic teeth and scaly eye sockets,
ridged, leathery wings. My bed knows them
as it knows cold nights filled with demons and hands,
my own
hands groping for some fabric otherworldly
and visceral, my angles bending
to a silenced geometry. Someone once said
that in Death's garden all the flowers are blue, but so
is remembering, the lingering aftertaste of a desire cooling
into corpse.

Ligeia's Despair

By winter I was dead
like tubers in the ground
left too long untouched
and rotting.

The loosening for my flesh,
toxic, left roots in soil
too venomous for even lyme.

You promised to sprinkle
Licorice seeds over my shell
because I loved blue

But soon, mourning clothes
became too heavy,
my pictures dust-skinned

And once a year something
in your mind said *seeds*. But
in a new bridal chamber

you had already forgotten
the twisting black ropes
the lonely-stained bones.

Bachelorettes

Vine tendrils sprouting from her skull, they are, small
ribbon springs, any number of helix.
She's turned away beside me, unshattered, all high
cheekbones and waterbright eyes for vox.

My own hair—a porcupine arrangement,
and two curved locks like scythes
to frame the oval of my face. So much dark in the hair
that it surrenders only to the red gore of lipsticked mouth.

Tonight we hunt for boys in bright mohawks,
the colored plumage of unapologetic scowl,
the only way to compromise—a shriek
not lost in noisy crowd.

Her Door Slamming in the Middle of the Longest Night

I never knew how to be concise with
you, how to be anything
but languor and lux and long
afternoons, with our twined limbs like
branches bowing to take hold of root.
I never knew how to be firm,
unbending felled twigs or milled lumber,
only, the reed bending and bending in
invitation to lean your wide mouth
over mine, stooping low enough to catch
me half-fallen.
I never knew how to be anything but
water, opening from a ripple's center
and parting wide the reflection
of the sunny leaf-spent lines,
casting mossy shadows like a soft nest for
nestled embraces.
Did she? Did she give you the stiff
slap of a wall where I was soil? Did she
ever know the silt beneath waves holds roots, too?

from Inside the Painted Window Frame

    1.

Sharp blades of morning filter through the dulling
slats of blinds.

I wake, weave my body on wrinkled sheets,
peel away on them layers of skin—

the *epidermis* and the *cutaneous* and the *fascias*—
idle breath, until nothing but bone remains.

Skeletal and limber so that pebble slips, skips
before me where I walk under bleaching sun.

The silken wind brings a starling wail down
like rain, or dry leaves—cloak for honest bone.

    2.

His heart: a jellyfish, soaking in the sun.
Endwise, it will be weighed
against the underworld of water, the fire,
against the sounds it has soaked.
A small coin floating in its center,
has turned duller than a copper moon.

    3.

A burst of red berries on the drying bush beside my door:
the green hill, a sacred mound: circled by winter wind,
my own whitening breath: every moment: hatching.

    4.

The way water slips down along an icicle,
adding another sheath of cold—

there is no subtlety like that in your kiss—

no shivering like a nascent stalactite learning how to harden.

I woke to a world sharper than light, waited
until the sun spilt like a seam of blood.

6.

The lurch
of the heart
is
not always love.

Mind the gap.

Before Solomon's Court

O, Hoopoe bird, lover of scent and frankincense and stone,
    grant me the vetiver green of your grassy soul
        to shield me from this sand's dazzling hoard.
I follow his throne to my own, but in your winged shadows,
    you hold the voiceless breath left trailing between homes.

Lovesick Wanderer, O Dervish of the Restless Heart

Whirling like the morning's salt-scented breeze, over soft dunes until the sandstorm tumult in me spins out unembraced across the whole of the horizon

Whirling like the wind over stark sandy dunes until the whole of me fills the horizon uplifting in maddening tumult, enraptured by the sun's face on every grain of time

Whirling like the rising and rising is a forever forgetting of a lightless descent into arid desert embrace, sand singing the whole of me to the skeletal skein of horizon

Exile

Fog descends on the tallest
of sky-troping towers, dissolving
them, leaving their roots
exposed,
reclaiming the geometry
of sky.
        This is the way snow
might look, falling upwards:
nepenthic.
           The union
of stratosphere & horizon
never so plain as in this:
the broad peopled world suspended
half in walking,
              half in dream.
Connected this way, not by thread
but breath, speech desists;
              distance
broken instead by measured glances,
wrapped in coat-sleeves, folded
                arms.
The spaces between & inside things
find voice,
          emerging from blood
cells, joints, molecules—listening
for the fall of exuvium beneath spent air.

A Swallow of Gravity

I carried with me a small smooth stone
from the beach. Something from the sea,
lent to me by my mermaid sister
far beneath
the turbulence of waves.
It is like silk
against the contours of my face, calm
as an egg now resting on my forehead.

White like the moon, like a pearl,
like the teeth of God.
Every perfect moment, broken
sediment.

If I don't take a coin
for the ferryman, will he let me stand
on the banks
and watch the faces of the dead? I will
take instead this pebble, drifting
with the tide
from my reach.

Talisman

Everywhere I look is turquoise

but I am not Julnar of the Sea
with a pearl big as the orb of her eye
in the coil of silver around her finger.

I wear the evil eye to still it, the silver
blade to wrench it from the watchers,
creeping, hooded, into my nightmares.

What is vision but a sense of sight?

their blind eyes and bone limb will ask,
for they are all iris as big as the face
and they speak through our tongues.

I am everywhere, turquoise, but I see.

The Reptile's Wife

Belly dance for me
in your second skin, slick as oil—
you stretch the vinyl well.

We dance like we fuck.

In your curves the year is 1785
& love is never fun
without the crime.

Eyes & mouth sly behind
that hair & you are slipping down,
down, drowning in the sight

of every way I'd like to cut you

loose into this dusk.
There are not enough days to forget
the guileless

sway of your hips, begging,
for a rope, to bind them
from a gaze like mine.

Animus: the Hierophant and the Hetaira

It is the monster behind the man
        that makes him   worth loving. Thick
heart   made from creature parts.
A life   of patchwork and shame. Give
him the hammer   and he breaks
your hand with it,   not to hurt,   but
to learn.   Because he has the same red
blood as you   who are gentle,   he is
immortal in his rage   —a true monster
is still beautiful beneath the rotten core—
and he will never learn   that guilt is not love.

Swampfed Lullaby

Morning was a lover's palm
firm against the small of back,
the bayou damp of the body.
Morning like lingering oaks
with branches low, enough
to lay my body on, open
to the sun. And, a body
in the green gray brownmuddy
swamp is always a pale thing,
pale as the crocodile's tooth,
reptilian, a rapist's hatchling
hands. It lies colder than
the sun it seeks, colder than
the marsh, just as soft. Open
to the looking. Morning was
a palm along the legs, and a vine
between them. Sun like a skin
left behind by the slither of the old
snake, now for the new. Morning
was an empty palm reaching
for green, grass thick like the song
of waning spring.

fury

Not lips—two magpies

facing eyes, pecking eyes & tails
upturned at edges.

No, not skin—a sheath
of maggots, split in seams like

myI, my eyes just rinds
of spoons, silvery, closed.

Close my eyes & I am closed
inside and night brings

moth wings stopping just short
of flame.

Give me a chameleon's coat instead,
scales like droplets of water

one beside another.
Not flame, not fluid shifting—

just the color of fire and bluing, I
will cease to burn.

Found Song

No words want to be spoken.
It is not the place of song or skull rattle.
Here is the hour of animal,

all fur
and teeth
and sex.

In the wilderness, I found
my barefoot soul in the mouth of Coyote,
the webs of Spiderwoman,

unfolding
in shadow on the path
before me.

The earth's voice
came from the cracks of quivering ground.
Love.

All things know how
to seek love.
So do you.

Unbalanced, hands open to keep apart

the woods
and
the sun.

Longing Along the Long Winter's Eve

Open your windows and open your doors and open your arms and open her arms into your arms and open your legs and open your mouth and open your sex and open your arms and open your legs and open your eyes to this blanketing dark-ness. Open your arms to the mask over your face. Open your own patchwork colored lens, logic left better in sleep and lucid dreams and. Open your hands and open your mind and your head and open your touch and your self, opening like this, oh, like this, like a petal, like a lotus, like a dew-drenched rose, like a thistle spilling nectar from the misty close of the open of the open of the lock of the lows. Open your windows and open your doors. In the open feel the open of the pages, yes the pages and the, oh, your pages open open like the petals left in honey and in dreaming and in lights like the others, like the shimmer of the stone-circled lights on the marshes and moors and the open doors and open yours...

Persephone in the Nights of Spring

There is a pit lodged in my solar plexus —[not an abyss, but a seedling]—
that you left there.

I can feel—[its slow unfurling, leaves as wide as the shadow of banana trees,
        stalks as tough, as tender as shipyard rope inside]—
the hard ridges of the stone. —[Is there an almond in the serrated shell
                      or an orchard of shelled bodies, an army
                      of ripening fruit ?]—

Around it, I am shrinking—[My blood thickens like syrup; I am drunk on it,
                    on the honeyed taste
                    of my own spit.]—

Take it out of me—[take this date seed, olive seed, plum seed from my center]—
until I am, again—[left with the blank of desire, the slow trickle of waiting.]—

Until I am thirsty for a seeded fruit without enough nectar to let me stop
at just one red grain.

Scrying for the Unworthy with Feather and Bone and Sanctuary

I: / falling into a swirling line of / falling into a / falling into innocence, there / is nothing more to say to you /nothing, at all. I don't / know you, I don't know / you, I don't know you in the way of this / I don't know this / life anymore. // Who we were is nothing more than skeletal and buried far beyond rot /or, melting. / You are your sickling garden, foliage and fallen. You are / The way you look at me, I see sockets of the dreamlands, only / where the remnants once became / true. // I can't / anymore / do this anymore, do / this without the strength of Atlas / the earthen world on my world on my worried shoulders / and not without the heart of Circe / witchy and willing / to take you / under / the blanching weeds. Not / every woman has the heart of / Penelope, after all. // I am going home, because / I am sung anymore / don't know where I'm from anymore / and the days / and the days are melting / beyond rot / into nothing but heat and flame and red, red suns that / flicker into catatonia. // The crocodiles are coming, with their greensick skins like vines. // This is wrong / this is /wrong, there is nothing / left to cling to in the chasm / the spirits pulling with / reptilian shadows/ at my ankles. There are hollows / left between us where the world once left / the hearts beside our unwashed feet. // The nightmare's just beginning in the heart of beasts and teeth / that hate / that chew. // Don't let it let / the stars consume me. Don't let the waters fill me with the empty / reach of something smaller than a pebble / or a pearl / sticking in your teeth / your devouring mouth, like hope / the edge of a hippopotamus roaring / from the heart of ancient fire.

Shade in the Telesterion, from Beyond the Mystery Rites of Eleusis in Spring

    [Of Things Done]

No, there are no
                    lights to show me the way,
but the moon has risen and the stars are bright.
Somehow, my feet know
                    just where to step and
                    just where to run.

I have been here before,
                    but not in this life. And I
have cried out into this dark
                    in some time before this time.

This altar's cold, I have known,
                    lain upon, layed upon, and lost.

This altar
         is the opening of my loss.
                  I waited there for a him
          who never
              came   for me, until
when he had gone, my spirit
              lingered.

I waited there.
         And, when…
they had gone.   He laid his fingers where
the knife had gone, head bowed
                to clear the altar cold with weeping.

Here, I see him, here
              I kiss him, here
I feel nothing
         but nothing is loss

I have been here before,
                  but not in this life. And I—
                              am I lost?

[Of Things Shown]

Descend, now, these dark stairs,
            these platforms steep,
            these tombstones within…
those oracle-dreamt and
            crumbled by dawn, a time ago.

Descend, now, deep,
            below the ground are remnants
                        of deeper fear,
                        of echoes
            fires in the fragments of this temple
and ghosts of long-dead gods still clinging to walls.

   [Of Things Known]

I own my marble
fingertips,
            they scrape away spectres in powder, in dust
            they make a paste of heartsick song into a hue
                        of lust, paint
                                    unlike the blank of ancient stone,
                        once something, then nothing, and now unknown.

When you sleep, dead to my song beneath the hum of barley,
                                                I will slip
            my fingernails underneath your eyelids—
            clean, smooth as letter-openers in my gesture—
I know the roads to trace onto your silent skeins,
                                    I will
trace roadways to cold altars and
      haunted ashes and
                  a place where death had come to life.

   [Of Things Told]

I shall meet you after incantations
                        in the place where—
Persephone crept out of Kykeon visions, green-robed,
      from under the cracks of earth and stone,

     pomegranate and peppered wheat, and
     the sorrowful sound of falling bone.

I know this altar, I know this low
       wailing moan
     that you will not remember, when you—
no, you will not remember when you wake to know this map
          lash laden in your flashes of white
gown and pomegranate red,
      limbs laden with another winter,
I remember,
   a time ago.

   [Of Things Done]

I remember white gowns stained red, and I remember
    the altar cold as death against
        the thousand silent-eyed,
         pilgrims weary and wise to rivers,
    twinned blue and black beneath the
        asphodels,
    the knowledge of a scythe against
       the thousand-silent, smiles of uneyed sight.

I will write into your sightless, some barrier of stone.

   [Of Things Given]

Your map, your feet will know the way, your step's guidance,
      your memory of—
Your restless footstep, stumbling,
        in search of processions long past spent in
panic and revelry, in the gathering of an unripened spring, in a procession
    with broken steps
    with grain
    with a shrouded veil, some palimpsest of vessels beating
     beneath unbroken skin.
A procession past the oracle stairs and the barrier of bodies
          turning
          away.

    [Of Things Foretold]

Come to the temple stair, the sacred stair, brave beyond centuries
       come to the broken pillar, the silent wall, come to the temple stair.
A time ago—come,
              there was he who left me there,
                            wrongspilt and unsplit..
Come to this cold beyond footstep and footstep and footstep
      come to this wail and this whirl, this stone, this embrace.
           Come to where you have been before,
                            but not in this life,
                              cried out into this dark
in some time before this time. The moon has risen and the stars are bright.

Aubade for a Seraph (or a Demon)

Wake with a dream, the dream he left you, knowledge of noetic names—
he, hierophant ancestral, seer of the ways, of spirit song—glyph
in your throat, a blackened hand, a leper's nose and murder
in the strangling hours when the sky hangs low, trees
bowing low, branches limbering in awe—

                                        You can ask, then,
for the angels, the thousands of birdwinged bodies without blood,
to still their thrum, to bring you
into a sheet behind a cloud's numb—
                            here, there are rooms, hidden
in wrinkles, in simple folds
                               here, the slippery skins will
never stop begging for more than is
                               here, the cold doesn't slip in
to the uncovered air just between your shoulderblades, or
the anxious curve of your hip,
                              where his hand warred once
                              broad, familiar, palmed, but now
                              somewhere else, faceless in time—

And even the shadows here have tongues, waiting to lick
the length of you, the creases of your ears, the lattice
of the corners of your eyes—afraid to close but too afraid to look
to one place—
               it was a hand there around your throat—
and it is a long time before sunrise.

Dream with Astrolabe and Compass

I filled my house with birdcages—antique—and lamps—tall, iron—and bits of bamboo—assembled into sculptures for the seating of some light. Drawing closed all the shutters, I waited for a luminescence that did not come. I wrapped my darkness in a shroud and shrouded the nascent suns, one by ones, and longed for the moon to emerge from the vetiver of dreams, filled with stones and green men and rockets—in path, fixed—and the sense that light could come from any of those distant radiant points, or from inside that darkness. I shuttered and shuddered and waited, until. The darkness yielded night and constellations of something distant enough and extinct enough and dead enough to tolerate. There—*Zubenelgenubi*. There—the eagle's head supernova. There—*Zubeneschamali*. There—the heart's nebula, a safe distance away in its crimson and its nostalgia, far enough away to break open a thousand and one pin-pricks of light and land as nothing but dust, coating the fabrics filling my house—some direction for the needle unaccustomed to aligning.

The Wanderer's Compass is a Quest to Find the House of God

And what of the blue cube above *Zubenelgenubi*? The southern claw of the scorpion or the tongue of the gentlemen? Does it carry the eclipsing shadow that will unfurl across the shadow of the moon? The planet orbiting like a lizard's eye around a 77th year of light originating in the sun – any sun, any star for that matter, a star whose matter may collapse its rays inward, boxed inside like a cube of light. A perfect blue squared square arcing beside the scorpion's claw to the *Zubeneschamali* of the scorpion's northern claw. And what of the tongue of the camel, lent to the language of the celestial like an astral cube in the constellated sky, turning face by face by face to say, simply *peace*.

Mirror Lake in Carlsbad Cavern Quivers Like a Scrying Glass Speaking

Blood Ibis, how long have you lived within
this breaking vessel, cardiac not corvid, not coward
not courage, but frozen in a bronzed votive
cast of fear once paralyzing all the scales and every coin
besides?

Blood Ibis, I am your wings of crimson
of scarlet of song and cry, clotting in my throat, this rush
of feathery flight
so congealing in my
unsung.

Down you swoop
and stab
and hold
while your span beckons the blank of sun—
Blood Ibis in the bright.

Ibis who are I and mine besides;
can you stop mid-fire
and mid-flight?
Give me the Ibis blood for my quill's
delight?

Self-Portrait as Wick-Tender and Candle Flame

I am half-starved at the root and stem by being
for another body
the wide opening petals of a plum-red peony.
He is salt-wind on a sailor's breath,
living on the ever-lit
flame of candle-wick in the window.
My nights are luminous with a far flame
that my face
cannot trope towards, cannot
diminish
though the fever in the darkness begs
to quench an uncertain glow.
Even a sailor can wear a halo
in a room across memory,
but a bloom is ill-spent in tending the solitary light;
the salt takes more thirst than an ocean-wave can heal.

Anthem for the Ancestors, O Dervish of the Restless Heart

(after the Kundiman & Kaya Press AWP Seattle Bruce Lee Party)

I don't have, for you, a Bruce Lee poem.

I don't have a poem about an elephant speaking
    in the voice of Ganesh.

I don't have the verse that versus the fundamentalist
    impulse to blow shit up that you don't like.

I don't have one foot in one land or one in another.

I don't know the name for myself that isn't diaspora.

I don't fit enough into one tongue or another,

    but I miss the tongue of that cowboy coming
    back home in a big truck,
    still smelling of fracking and the fuel fields.

I don't have, for you, a poem on the occasion of the
    owning of the race of the racists.

I don't have a voice stifled for you beneath an unchosen veil.

I don't have, for you, words that speak your language.

I don't have, for you, words that say "approval"—not
    from home, nor from home away from home,
    either.

I don't have, for you a poem, about the nation of my
    name,

    ———just the sinewy sibilance of my fingers,
    scratching out sighs on a page,

    while I think of that good ole once upon a cowboy
    saying, "I don't really read such books that often,"

all the while reading stories on my skin, his fingers
writing silence

        on my sunbrowned sin, and

my thoughts reaching out to hold his bearded face,
pull his hips close to mine so that I am filled with a

forgetfulness of words that I cannot name, or
unlearn how to say.

Those places he has been, I have not; he has seen
the sands that gave me my name,
                Kan yama kan, Qaf and beyond.

I do not have for you a poem about the nomad in my blood
    that knows these sandsongs that I cannot, do not
    know how, to say—

    Oh, tie-ers of knots, untie my tongue, unknot what
I do not have, for you, a poem about.

But for The Garden Is The Guardian Ravenous

Some hours till dawn by the side of a road with spent heart. What the want doesn't is a light on a highway lined by night, by bright-needled cacti, by a moonblood lingering on the gloaming gravel of an unromantic interlude past abandoned by the long-set sun. A space like a breath held in. What hole there cowers, filled with toe-thick ants and a scorpion's black tongue, isn't a scarab-scented vista but a horizon for a starfield, fading through my earthen skin. Stones, standing under the breath of darkness. What field goes undone is as open as the sun's distant perilhelion. Mapped, unmapped, unwandered like a nomad caught in the buried, hollow sounds of the unsung sands beyond his sight. Do his dunes sing louder as the longing lingers, inching into lucid-bright the bedouin's waking dream? Do the ocotillo bloom before his sight? Like her, blossoming grass, like her wailing, a keening, a creeping, a crocodile's low and languid crawl? Starstone. Seed against darkness. A pepper jasmine's breeze. Does the body give its breath at last, to hours spilling open and unstoppered? Shadow-borne agarwood, oudh and vetiver, scar-won myrrh, the lingering attar of oasis rose. What lines the unmapped is the inkthick carapace of the cartographer's lust, clotting in the moonlit brush, the desert rising to nightsong. What the want doesn't is a beam, rising like river water over a flat plain, over a tangle, a breath in the cold, over grain like the bleached bones of orbit, unrelenting, duneless, dry with howling. What is longing but a blooming in the blood? Like this. A distillate wish of a rhizome's rooting in wet clay, a remembrance of water, flowing pools from the caverns of the court of vines, heady with the beckoning susurrus of petals underfoot.

Nor Equinox Nor Promise

If the tide is right and the moon is high enough to carry these waves to shore,

If the boat's tether is knotted loose and its anchor is gone and its oars are wide enough to part the crests of these waves as they reach the shore,

If Kilbirnie Kirk there is full of light by stars and by candles and by lanterns that skim off of these wet peaks and part the dark enough to carry this boat along to shore,

If the green of the hills falls through the moon's reflection in the loch and opens a passage on the boat for those who might travel these waves to shore,

If the high ways are clear of men in the hillshades and the boat seats two in secrecy, their shadows discretely long along the moon's light as it moves along these crests that reach the shores of the other side,

If the rope is untied,

    If the boat is still, without broken boards,

If,

    If the boat's wood is dark as the loch,

If the oars fit rough hands,

If you come to this green place, sung by the gone, by the there where the wild roses grow and the moss blankets the stones, beside the sound of the waves and the waves on the waves on the way high along the way to the shore,

If you wear your mourning black and your beads of jet round your darkening throat and your darkling hair, shining darkly the moon and the mossy and the roses back into the night,

If you shimmer in your rosy skin, in the thistle-bright sheen of the moon's milk face on your moss-given stride,

If you cast your glance aside, behind the fae hum of the night's dark shade,

If you rose, stone as cold by the fair bell of the moon's light across the way,

If on the other side of that shore is a new tether, a new anchor, a new rope, nae a footpath made of old stone and rune stone and an archway not to a land of bones, if

References and Notes

[Chalked Circles and Circumferences of Breath]
The 14th Dalai Lama said, in a 1985 ceremony, that "Shambhala is not an ordinary country...We can only say that it is a pure land, a pure land in the human realm." In the mid 1300s, Ibn Battuta walked 730,000 miles on foot, more than 29 times the earth's circumference (24901.55 miles), chronicling his travels, before returning to his journey's beginning. Many surmised that he returned only after finding Shambhala. In various Islamic folk traditions, people will recite a prayer and blow a circle of air around the person for whom protection and safe passage is sought, unbroken by speech until after the wish for safety is fully expressed around the person's being.

[Amphibious Catalogue with Invisible Stair,]
Melusine, a feminine water spirit of springs and rivers, is a figure from folklore from whom some royalty had once claimed lineage, especially the French rulers of Cyprus in the 13th century. She is often depicted as having wings or a mermaid's tail, or both. She has appeared in early medieval pilgrimage-based travel writing, as a woman who is cursed into the shape of a dragon and who is seeking the release of a kiss that will change her back into human form permanently.

[A Lover's Quarrel]
Pierrot and Columbine are figures in Commedia dell'Arte and pantomime. They are lovers involved in a triangle who represent the dangers of trust, betrayal, seduction, and the deathly. Columbine is also the name of a blue meadow flower.

[Predatory]
The bracketed lines include overheard snatches or misheard lyrics of songs. The poem intends these references as a scavenger hunt of sorts, inviting a search for the songs and then a listening of those lines in those places that feel like a sound sampled into the lyric. Songs referenced by these lines have been performed by Bella Morte, VNV Nation, The Cruxshadows, Iris, Miranda Sex Garden, Bjork, DJ Octagon, The Smiths, and REM.

[Meditation After a Lost Battle: Curatorial Statements for a Museum Exhibit]
In various Sufi traditions, Sema, or whirling in trance, is associated with meditative and contemplative remembrance of God. It can be accompanied by percussion or chanting. Rumi, as famous for his poetry as for the whirling dervishes that he has inspired, suggests that Sema is for the restless of heart, that it is a window toward the rosegarden of the beloved, through which the seeker may catch a glimpse of it. He once famously said, "Does the moth think about the flames? For Love's spirit, thought is a disgrace. When the warrior hears the sound of the drum, at once he is worth ten thousand men."

[Before Solomon's Court]
In Islamic folklore, the Hoopoe bird brought the Queen of Sheba to King Solomon's Court where she discovered her own throne, transported there by djinni under the command of the King to demonstrate his power. The Hoopoe bird features prominently as a guide in Farid ud'Din Attar's mystical Islamic tale in verse, *The Conference of the Birds*.

[Oil Field. Mine, field. Afghanistan.]
Afghanistan was famous for its pomegranates long before it was famous for the wars waged on its soil. Pomegranates in general have significance in many ancient traditions, including the Greek in which they are associated with Persephone as the fruit of the dead, the Semitic in which they are associated with Moses and fertility, in religious Christian decorative imagery associated with Jesus, in religious Muslim depictions of the gardens of the afterlife as the fruits of Paradise, and in many cultures across Asia rooted in Persia, India, and China as representations of luck, prosperity, and fertility.

[Siren Song]
While the Sirens in Homer's *Odyssey* are famous for their seductive wiles, it is less commonly known in popular culture that hearing the siren's mantic song bears a particular danger: those who hear it will not be welcomed in their homes and domestic spheres or ever feel at peace there, doomed to restlessness; this consequence may be particularly troubling for those soldiers returning from the Trojan War depicted in the *Iliad* and longing for return to home and domestic life after the perils of such a long war. Sirens are sometimes depicted as mermaids, but also depicted as companions of Persephone with wings (not unlike Melusine) in the works of Ovid.

[A Poultice for the Reckoner of Time and Seasons]
In Ancient Egyptian mythology, Ibis-headed Thoth, who is generally known as the Scribe of the Gods who is the keeper of law and knowledge of the navigation of humanity's paths through the universe, is also known as the Reckoner of Time and Seasons. He is associated with records of souls who pass into the afterlife with pure hearts past Ammit, the Eater of Hearts and the Devourer of the Dead, a demonness and funerary deity who is part hippopotamus, part lion, and part crocodile.

[Ligeia's Despair]
Ligeia is the name of a character in a story of the same name by Edgar Allan Poe. The character believes that life is sustained by willpower and after her death, her spirit returns to inhabit and transform a future wife of her former husband. Reclaiming love from the afterlife was a common motif in the ancient world, as well, most often associated with the mythical Persephone and her mother Demeter and with Orpheus and Eurydice.

[Talisman]
Talismans and amulets are common among the folklore of the Islamic world, which privileges the idea that deliberate remembrance of God can cure many ills and that to carry an object bearing the word of God can assist in such remembrance. These items feature prominently in Sufi stories as well as in the famous *Thousand Nights and One Night* (also known as the *Arabian Nights*), in which we encounter a character named Julnar of the Sea, who is, essentially, a mermaid. Turquoise is a stone that is often engraved with devotional words, such as might be found on a religious talisman. It was also associated with Ancient Egypt, Arabia, and Mesopotamia alongside the deeper blue Lapis Lazuli, which is found there, too. In India and Persia, Turquoise is associated with luck, affording good luck to some and bad luck to others.

[Aubade for an Absent Lover, or From the Asphodel Fields]
The mythical Asphodel Fields are made up of pallid, ghostly flowers most often associated with the Greek Underworld and with the neutrality of a good life rather than with the rewards of valor, but also referenced by other names in Ancient Egyptian and Near Eastern lore.

[Dream With Astrolabe and Compass]
Zubenelgenubi and Zubeneschamali are Arabic names for stars in famous constellations. They are associated with the scorpion's claws, as well as the scales of justice. The latter is known as Beta Librae and is known as the brightest star in the zodiac constellation of Libra. The former, also known as Alpha Librae, is actually a twin star in the zodiac constellation of Libra that is brighter than our sun; it rises and sets with our sun around Halloween, each year. They are now commonly associated with Libra, but were once associated with the constellation Scorpius, the former being the Southern Claw of the Scorpion and the latter being the Northern Claw of the Scorpion.

[Mirror Lake in Carlsbad Caverns Quivers Like a Scrying Glass Speaking]
Mirror Lake is a subterranean drip-pool formation in the Big Room of the Carlsbad Caverns fed by surface water, situated near a formation of stalactites called Fairyland. A sign marking the Lake was written in mirror writing script so that it could be read in the reflection of the lake. Artworks of Arabic Calligraphy also often utilized mirror writing in conjunction with palindromic ornamentation and geometric patterning.

[Shade in the Telesterion, from Beyond the Mystery Rites of Eleusis in Spring]
The Telesterion, near Athens is one of the sites of the ancient mystery cult of Demeter and Persephone. Initiation Rituals were conducted under a vow of secrecy each year in Spring in the Eleusinian Mysteries; participants in these rites were said to lose fear of death. They included things shown, things done, and things said, which together were considered the unrepeatable, on penalty

of death. Many scholars assert that the potency of these mysteries involved the entheogenic agent borne in a ritual drink known as Kykeon, which may have enabled psychedelic experiences. The festivities included sacrifices, dancing, feasting, procession, pilgrimage, and revelry. We know much surrounding the events, but very little about the rites themselves. Aleister Crowley created a related series of rites based on seven classical planets of importance to antiquity, which he claimed would induce religious ecstasy in audience members, calling them "The Rites of Eleusis;" these brought Crowley and his spiritual organization ∴A∴A∴, which focused on "scientific illuminism," into the public eye.

[O Dervish of the Restless Heart]
The typical Arabic tale involves magic and conjuring, even in its framework, and it traditionally begins not with "Once Upon a Time," with a focus on historicity or temporal particularity that has since been passed by, but outside of time with "Kan Ya Makan," meaning "There was, and there was not" or, perhaps "Now you see it, now you don't" as the common parlance might suggest, placing the story outside of time and space and at one with reality, at once. It is used frequently in *The Thousand Nights and One Night*. In Persian lore, Koh-e-Qaf, or just Qaf, is known as Fairyland and in some tales as the Mountain Sanctuary of the Demons. In Farid ud'Din Attar's *Conference of the Birds*, the avian collective goes to the mythical Qaf in search of the Simurgh, or Phoenix bird, only to discover the secret that Simurgh means "si murgh" or "thirty birds" which are essentially the collective who have gone to seek the Master and have found something of the divine within themselves. The poet Kahlil Gibran of Lebanon once referred to the beauty of the land as that of a bride in springtime, filled with the allure of *houris*, or like a mermaid basking in the glow of the star that sustains us. The following lines adapted from *The Song of Solomon* (4:10-5:2), are worth considering in the context of this series: "How much better is your love than wine! And the fragrance of your oils than spice! Your lips, O my Bride, drop as the honeycomb, honey and milk under your tongue, and the smell of your raiment is like the smell of Lebanon. / A garden shut up is my Bride, a spring shut up, a fountain sealed. / Your shoots are an orchard of pomegranates, with perilous fruits; henna with spikenard plants and saffron, calamus and cinnamon, with all trees of frankincense, myrrh and aloes, with all the chief spices. You are a fountain of gardens, a well of living waters and flowing streams. / Awake, O North Wind, and come you south; blow upon my garden that the scent of spice may rise aloft. Let my beloved come into his garden and eat his fruits. / I am come into my garden, my spouse, gathered my myrrh with my spice, eaten my honeycomb with my honey. I have drunk milk with my wine. O beloved, I sleep, but my heart wakes: it is the voice of my beloved that knocks." The story of King Solomon and the Queen of Sheba is found in Jewish, Christian, and Islamic traditions alike, though it varies slightly in each.

[FONTS]

The poems utilize Lucida Blackletter in the titles and FootlightMT Light in the text. Blackletter is a script whose heyday of usage was 1150 to the 17th century; forms of it were used to print the Gutenberg Bible, as well as works of Chaucer. The type's calligraphic influences reflected social attitudes through Latin Type, and enabled print's popularization; at the same time, Arabic Calligraphy flourished by hand, rather than movable type, and modern versions reflect these shifts. It served as a precursor to more geometrically inspired designs like Didot and Footlight. The Lucida version was developed by Bigelow and Holmes in 1992. FootlightMT is an irregular serif typeface developed by Ong Chong Wah in 1985, with the intent to combine elegant, authoritative craftsmanship with theatrical sparkle; its italic weight was developed before its regular version, lending an old-world flair to a modern font. In a way, the relationship between the heritages of Blackletter and Footlight evokes, in book art visual metaphor, the relationship between imagining a thing and fixing it in the world, saying a thing aloud and fixing it onto the page, that influence the production of the poems in this book.

Acknowledgements

The author gratefully acknowledges the publications, individuals, and organizations that have supported the work of this book:

"Beware: Alligators Do Not Feed Ducks" and "Talisman" in *Tahzeeb e Deccan*.

"Oil Field. Mine, Field. Afghanistan." in *Voices of Resistance: Muslim Women on War, Faith, & Sexuality*. Editor: Sarah Husain (Seal Press).

"Dusk Intermediary," "Nor Equinox Nor Promise," "An Architecture for Mystery" in *The Offending Adam*.

"Self-Portrait with Wick-Tender and Candle Flame" and "Amphibious Catalogue with Invisible Stair," in *The Loudest Voice Anthology. (Vol. 1)*. Editors: Amaranth Borsuk, Bryan Hurt, and Genevieve Kaplan (Figueroa Press).

"Chalked Circles and Circumferences of Breath", "Demon: Lover," "Aubade for a Seraph (or a Demon)," "Aggregate," "An Architecture for Mystery," "Nor Equinox Nor Promise" in my chapbook *Of the Divining and the Dead* (Finishing Line Press).

"Shock & Awe" and "Longing Along the Long Winter's Eve" in *Political Punch: Contemporary Poems on the Politics of Identity*. Editors: Erin Elizabeth Smith and Fox Frazier-Foley (Sundress Publications).

"O Dervish of the Restless Heart," containing "Anthem for those Ancestors," "American Dream with Horizon and Pomegranate," and "Lovesick Wanderer, O Dervish of the Restless Heart," was nominated for a Rhysling Award in the Long Poem category. It was also nominated by Zoetic Press for the 2016 Independent Best American Poetry Award, and it won: "Anthem for those Ancestors" was published in the 2016 *Independent Best American Poetry* anthology edited by Steve Fellner (GOSS183 Publishing House).

Earlier versions of the poems "Dream with Astrolabe and Compass," "Door Slamming in the Middle of the Night," "Gilded," "Once," "Like Red, Dancing for the Wolf," "Pantomime: A Palindrome for Beauty," "A Lover's Quarrel," "Ever Aftering," "Fossil Before the Making," "Self-Portrait as Wick-Tender and Candle Flame," and "Longing Along the Long Winter's Eve" appear in my chapbook *Limerence* (Chax Press).

Carol Muske-Dukes, David St. John, & Susan McCabe at the University of Southern California; Naomi Shihab Nye, Khaled Mattawa, Judith Kroll, &

Thomas Whitbread at the University of Texas in Austin; Eamonn Wall & Fidel Fajardo-Acosta at Creighton University. The Virginia C. Middleton Fellowship at The University of Southern California; The James A. Michener Fellowship at The University of Texas; The Fania Kruger Fellowship at the University of Texas; The writing fellowships granted by The University of Southern California and their English, Literature and Creative Writing Departments.

And acknowledges, with gratitude and love, the magnanimous support of family, friends, and writing community in the creation and production of this book: my parents Tahir & Abida Syed Razvi, Shehla Razvi and Babak Mobasheri, Suemyra Razvi and Mustafa Syed, Musa, Iliyah, Zachariah, Mubeen, Mahir, my fearless editrix and friend Fox Frazier-Foley, Jilly Dreadful, Mary Field, Cody Todd, Neil Aitken, Josie Sigler, J Barager, Suraj Shankar, Jess Piazza, Kelli Anne Noftle, Amaranth Borsuk, Genevieve Kaplan, Alexis Lothian, Katy Karlin, Yetta Howard, Janalynn Bliss, Mark Marino, Lee Ann Gallaway, Farid Matuk, Carrie Fountain, Anna Rosen Guercio, Tim Wong, Diana Arterian, Diana Lopez, AJ Ortega, Charles Alexander, Kyle Schlesinger, Margaret Rhee, Leah Maines, Percival Everett, TC Boyle, Mark Irwin, Dana Johnson, Aimee Bender, and Lauren A. Pirosko, who has mad design skills!, and so many more that I haven't been able name here from among my family and friends and community.

About the Author

Saba Syed Razvi is currently an Assistant Professor of English and Creative Writing at the University of Houston in Victoria, TX. Her poems have appeared journals such as *The Offending Adam, Diner, TheTHE Poetry Blog's Infoxicated Corner, The Homestead Review, NonBinary Review, 10x3 plus, 13th Warrior Review, The Arbor Vitae Review,* and *Arsenic Lobster,* among others, as well as in anthologies such as *Voices of Resistance: Muslim Women on War Faith and Sexuality, The Loudest Voice Anthology, The Liddell Book of Poetry, Political Punch: Contemporary Poems on the Politics of Identity,* and the *2015 Independent Best American Poetry* anthology. She's been honored by James A. Michener, Fania Kruger, and Virginia C. Middleton Fellowships. She earned a PhD in Literature & Creative Writing at the University of Southern California. Her chapbook of poems titled *Of the Divining and the Dead* was published by Finishing Line Press in 2012, and her chapbook of poems titled *Limerence* is forthcoming from Chax Press in 2016. Her poems have been nominated for the Best of the Net Award, the Rhysling Award, and have won a 2015 Independent Best American Poetry Award. These days, in addition to working on scholarly research on interfaces between Science and contemporary Poetry, she is studying Sufi Poetry in translation, and writing new poems and fiction.

A Note on the Type

From the brilliant hoard of coin and heavy / citadel's keep, the uninitiated mystic falters / through the forest memoried along the seething / banks of river, emerging / bare bodied and bare handed into the flaying / sun of this desert. The oasis appears, ever / alighted, a fortress under the shimmer of fire-shade. / In its courtyard are stems and spines reptilian, scaled, sharp-edged. / The unaligned / gnostic, draped bare in borne promise / steps onto the banks and emerges golden / as a crocodile accustomed to basking / like a basilisk or a butterfly's antenna. / Her teeth grow sharp and, hungry, / she pulls from the tree's fronds a string of glittering flesh, flayed from the resinous / taste; as it falls / in loops and coils, the mystic begins to learn / the reading of the shadows and light blooming from inside, / lucid letters of black and bright thorn, budding fruit haunting the reflection / of these vines. As she clambers / along the banks, the oasis fades, and her / wet, taloned feet leave prints light and pallid, crisp in their / movements onto the blank horizon of the beyond, a page / waiting to be filled / with the lucid black letters of gilded / blade in ribbons, fallen / from a maw turning back to a mannish mouth, // the light foot / printing the metered step, / measuring from man's stride to a woman's lilting song. The seeker / speaks in many tongues: / a song hangs in the air, haunts / pulp of plant and seed, and leaves / bearing the palimpsest of her angling, inkly gait, her / chiromancy of a heritage clutched from clay and fire, // waterspent unearthly light.

A Note on the Setting of the Type:

From within the crocodile's keep,

I have emptied myself hollow—

I am left.
               With the echo
of you,
        your words left.

           Split me open
with a drop of sound
                     like a spike,
slither in an open cave,

        a desert of nothing but snow.

Leave me—
            brittle,
bare and bonestrung—
                  a lute.
Leave me to long—

Is my heart a stone
               or, a geode—
filled with stones,

               candy-hued crystalline teeth,
prismed, longing
               to reflect the light
left,
     instead
               of holding its echo?

www.ingramcontent.com/pod-product-compliance
Lightning Source LLC
Chambersburg PA
CBHW071745080526
44588CB00013B/2160